Borderline Fortune

W9-CEW-464

The National Poetry Series was established in 1978 to ensure the publication of five collections of poetry annually through five participating publishers. The Series is funded annually by Amazon Literary Partnership, William Geoffrey Beattie, the Gettinger Family Foundation, Bruce Gibney, HarperCollins Publishers, The Stephen and Tabitha King Foundation, Padma Lakshmi, Lannan Foundation, Newman's Own Foundation, Anna and Olafur Olafsson, Penguin Random House, the Poetry Foundation, Amy Tan and Louis DeMattei, Amor Towles, Elise and Steven Trulaske, and the National Poetry Series Board of Directors.

THE NATIONAL POETRY SERIES

WINNERS OF 2020 OPEN COMPETITION

Borderline Fortune by Teresa K. Miller
Chosen by Carol Muske-Dukes for Penguin Books

Requeening by Amanda Moore
Chosen by Ocean Vuong for Ecco

[WHITE] by Trevor Ketner
Chosen by Forrest Gander for University of Georgia Press

Philomath by Devon Walker-Figueroa
Chosen by Sally Keith for Milkweed Editions

Dear Specimen by W. J. Herbert
Chosen by Kwame Dawes for Beacon Press

ALSO BY TERESA K. MILLER

POETRY

sped

Forever No Lo

NONFICTION

Food First: Selected Writings from 40 Years of Movement Building

(coeditor)

PENGUIN BOOKS

Borderline Fortune

Teresa K. Miller

PENGUIN BOOKS
An imprint of Penguin Random House LLC
penguinrandomhouse.com

Copyright © 2021 by Teresa K. Miller
Penguin supports copyright. Copyright fuels creativity, encourages diverse
voices, promotes free speech, and creates a vibrant culture. Thank you for
buying an authorized edition of this book and for complying with copyright
laws by not reproducing, scanning, or distributing any part of it in any form
without permission. You are supporting writers and allowing Penguin to
continue to publish books for every reader.

Page 71 constitutes an extension of this copyright page.

LIBRARY OF CONGRESS CATALOGING-IN-PUBLICATION DATA
Names: Miller, Teresa K., author.
Title: Borderline fortune / Teresa K. Miller.
Description: New York : Penguin Books, [2021] | Series: Penguin poets |
Includes bibliographical references.
Identifiers: LCCN 2021008296 (print) | LCCN 2021008297 (ebook) |
ISBN 9780143136811 (paperback) | ISBN 9780525508304 (ebook)
Subjects: LCGFT: Poetry.
Classification: LCC PS3613.I5585 B67 2021 (print) |
LCC PS3613.I5585 (ebook) | DDC 811/.6—dc23
LC record available at https://lccn.loc.gov/2021008296
LC ebook record available at https://lccn.loc.gov/2021008297

Printed in the United States of America
        1st Printing

Set in Adobe Garamond Pro
Designed by Ginger Legato

For my family—
here, gone, chosen

CONTENTS

Borderline Fortune

I

Of the Dead

who were you?

Merely a kid keeping alive.

—Anne Sexton

I came here to conjure you.
What may I say—
anything, all of it, friction
on the flint, many-armed agent
of entropy. What wrath would
I risk reaping, what disowning.

Who bore me
to the shore, pressed
me under, dragged there
ragged gasps.

If I am already orphaned, why fear
orphaning, this splintered boom in my hand.

What I built better than what
you offered me, my first sin.
Erasure only takes
a generation—we'll be cursed
and blessed this way.

I woke a forest. What sounds serene
has a rotten floor. I could dress it up, candles

on the sundered trunks, silk scarves and cut
flowers. But you arrive already

cleaving, a riven nausea in the cambium,
some needle-leafed private anguish.

The canopy swoons. You could hypnotize yourself
a savior, nourish a legacy in your suckers

and saplings, bank on a lightning-struck
triple crown. Topple early and end it.

I never had a sister. I had a girl
who threw a brick at my head.

I never had a brother but a fellow traveler,
warped melancholy by our raising, queer like me.

Later, no one. All the mortals on the stoop—
how to revive them, usher them in.

I lift the ban—if you are gone,
you will speak your own language.

You broke my mother and so you broke
me, lost in the thicket of your misfortune.

Sharp brittle branches sticky with birdshit,
dusted with gray down.

If I had a child, she was already mine. We did it backward, skipping time.

The mouth of the Duwamish smells like creosote. Gravel yard. Freight train on a rusted trestle.

We lashed a raft together and set off paddling. I wasn't yet born. The water dried salty, reliable—cold.

In the game, if you get good news,
if you get bad news, if you've driven
in traffic, you're tired, the lazy
afternoon grows too boring, too hot,
if you're lonely, if the neighbors
are married, the garden overgrown,
if your friend is sick, if your daughter calls,
take a drink.

Summer-gray night, my unprotector
slumbered among the ants. I cleaned
her frosted paces from the entry,
through the kitchen, mapping her descent.

Sometimes, a little drunk,
I want a baby, too. The horizon
where you surrender your first vision,
pass the currented point
and keep swimming, the wish
you'd unwhisper.

I fell from the roof but could not crack.
Sank past the seawall but would not drown.
Ripped open my arm, but the worst
part of me would not bleed.

The river drew a breath—
I heard it whipping up the gorge,
almost threw me from my ledge.

I drank gasoline but would not light.
Dug a hole in my throat yet found
no sound. Even mute,
you hunted me.

I'm asking you to believe in what you've never seen or heard—
still, listen, it will save you. Don't misunderstand: No personal

god will resurrect to offer grace, no reward waits
on the other side of suffering. Instead, imagine

your skull dissolved, not your temporal armor but the rampart
you think you stare from. No longer the sound of the bird's chirp

or the car passing but movement in the plane
where your head used to be. Can you find that place? She will

swing from her bough, but you'll have nothing left to break.

Who were we thawed,
rebounding from retreated glaciers?

You were snow on the red tile porch
outliving your generation, holding fast
the prophecy of your death in gnarled stick fingers.
Resisting the melt until August,
then sublimating into air.

Along the way, more than one
will renounce you, refusing
to say why. Your solace will smash
to a bony pulp, go lifeless.
The afterimage, your father's
furrowed brow unwinding a trail—
you'll ascend the last hundred
feet scrambling against columnar
basalt, against vertigo, Pacific spit's
hooked tail below the mountain
your ancestors stole.

Was hope a thing with feathers?
I think it rested densest carbon,
a small, stubborn shard.

Who wanted the glint.
I saved myself two years
dormant in the ground,
bare root, longer—part of me
remains asleep.

I looked back and you were unqueened—
sudden, without ceremony,

afraid of me.

When did our tormenters become
so frail, pock-marked shell fragment,
grain of sand.

Past whittling
the moment,
we go underground,

the dead murmuring in memory.
Once, the canyons were born, once,
every river had a first day to flow.

Once, I rose a blank sandstone
canvas and you scratched
your name
in my side.

Staggered down the shivering fossil seep, an ancient
unearthed stream murky with our skin and sweat.
What withered life I worry inside me,
a Frankenstein montage. The dinosaur halfway to flight
claws against intercostals, tapping on ribs
too late, too late, too late.

II

Our Own Worst Consequence

I was cowering at the circumference
Of your heart, howling

—Lucie Brock-Broido

Until the magnetic pole reverses,
no amount of trying will summon
you a mother. Until the Arctic ice
returns to its sheets and the calving
thunder cracks backward. Haul
yourself out,
one frozen leg at a time.

From the corpse-sized pillar,
Noguchi called forth
rings of a worm, strikes
like sticks of dynamite.

How far the gale carried us
to get tangled in our own string.
A whole continent. A separate
ocean.

In Queens, I am a stone
carved to let water
run down. My heart
has stopped. The stones
envy my stillness.

Dregs cast, camper top
torn and bent in the shadow,
the continent's highest peak,
towns of circling corvids, junctions,
ghosts.

How will I learn your chaos

never sprang
from me, wasn't mine,
this pile of pointless rubble.

Bolting dandelion, buttercup,
ground ivy, proud and purple, dried
and on the wind before I got wise.

Chopped back into the grass,
now a fixture in the landscape.

Though I doubt another life
will bring a reckoning, what good
does it do to wish you
poor,
found out, abandoned
in this one.

The branches sang me silent. Papery maple
skittered on the window. Cutting too hard

too fast spurs a reaction in kind. My creator
topped them all. Thirty winters thrust

through summer, I clenched my swallowed octaves.
You twirled me a crackling helicopter, chased me a birch

twig broom. It wasn't all bad, was it. Didn't we in the slant
light have fun.

Then, you see only the knot,
learn to name every place the string
bends, turns and dives toward the core.
Stop pulling. Find your hands
occupied elsewhere.

I dissolved
They would act upon me
I was what proof
I thought the rainy bunker of a chiton
Her embrace appeared a whetted oyster shucker
We waded out hurling geoducks, harvesting

Any we is an eye in the pearl's center
Knife-winged solitude, a trinket for your witness

Now what will you take from me?
Breeze flapping the sheets, rock slaps
the creek. Will I ever stop reassembling
what never rent. You swept
through, gust at the screen door,
left me beating.

The maybe possible flared out, bottom of an hourglass,
but I couldn't fit through the waist. We laid,

we overdosed. My disintegrating ally stole
tools to buy poison—I saw her works

but not her face. Relief just another anteroom,
an empty-weathered theme park.

For years, I watched water lap

the basement, tar oozing between white
tiles, cockroaches like gilling knives.

We stomped them and they'd stand up, crocodilian,
scurry away. You said I was too direct,

especially for a woman, but what direction, fractures
spilling out this chipped mouthful.

Rift in your tooth and veins in your shell
already ruptured well before you emerged—
you clutched them around you, a jagged quilt.

Remembrance branching like a pitchfork turns
and tosses the villains. You cower,
but they will pile beneath the cherry tree,
make black, rich soil.

The future hangs in panicles, yet
we are frostleaf and final, falling.

What am I if not a meadow, a rat
tunneling through the scraps, a pair
of starlings quarreling over too much seed.

Where you are beyond the glass is not
the real game, our strides
unreconciled, our ties
too loose.

You unspooled five thousand promises,

I wound them up, a pitted anchor,
a counterweight.

Truth tempts
banishment. Finish this tale
before braiding a prettier one.

I recoil from the howling, the same lonely
wolfdog penned another day. What can I give you,

sleepless and fluttering. By the time you realize you're alive,
this is your life, the light already cooled toward evening.

Forever and nothing. Which drooping river birch will you sacrifice,
what muddy vinca-covered bank fending off the ivy.

I don't listen for you now, your crow step,
so eager to say my own piece. How does it

start. The ants came to tear my house down.
I went to bed thinking of them, woke plotting

against them. I did not dream. A legion of men
that summer, none could bear to let me

speak. They focused over my shoulder,
the vacant corner a more willing

conspirator. Where will I lay you, wright,
smith, climber cutting to the node, choosing

a new leader.

If you are the hawk, fly higher
than the bolas. If you walk the ground,
leave the weapon by your side.
Together, you whip a twisted figure
crashing, caught in your sinew
and reason.

Two nights I tumbled from the ladder.
Then what I grasped could not scare me,
though we swayed up the dripping dark,
calcified deer skeleton, the jungle
and its leeches, leafy silhouetted
sinkhole in the skylight. The fantasy
had a weight, a mass we hefted
but could not take home.
Maybe thigh-deep in lake mud
I will hear you, you will tell me.

Lured back, I spun myself a shiny aluminum wing—

but in the afternoon, she put on a new face.
Those you love will evaporate before you, leave

their slack-jawed wind-up bodies lying in the yard.
Nicotine-stained filters reeking in the kitchen garbage.

Here is the next moment of your life: You spent it
in my crooked song.

In the end, there was no end.
You limp along coated in ash
glowing like radiation or starlight.
I won't know which until you go.
Besides, they are the same.

So long I chased the resolution—
how to make concrete feel remorse, swifts
change course, bulbs will themselves
not to bloom. You'll leave
one more unfinished row.

III

Disenthrall

you can feel the presence
of a possible otherwhere.

—Lucille Clifton

The same road awaited. Someday came
to set out walking.

A whirling turnkey toy in the night circus,
one Polaroid replacing the hours

no man or child would save you.
Your weather

came to waste you. How I yearned
to claim a new ecosystem,

that dry stand of beetle kill pine.

We do not resolve. The ceiling caves in other
ways, sighing through its transmutation.

To rise, I wandered underland. We embarked
through the matoa, fog-thick, slick,

and tedious except in the sharpest places.
Fretted, passed ourselves hand to hand.

A valley with a roof, a crypt blueshifted,
a novel muddle we brighten to ferry aloft.

When would each shattered knuckle
reform and tuck away its denser

secret? When at last you became
a gutter luring water from the door.

When you rose, a skin boat on the ice floe.
The pinnacle a foothill, the trumpets heralding

fermata, muffled crow.

I inherited not a house, but the memory
of a house. The stranger camouflaged,

stretched shadow before breaching the cellar,
white paint grit-stained.

We cannot ever be alone. Broad day,
rain mixed with snow. No harm,

no me for two generations, no place
I could touch except in sleep to say

at last *but I didn't live here.* So my dragon
was a paper lantern, never even wild.

When the moth-eaten phantoms tire,
may we choke ourselves awake.

Any no one could play this hollow interloper
who tells you to transform—your frame outfitting

itself, inverting triangular. You in your own
scapulae, over-honed, over-knowing,

your byline too modernist and should change.
Hear that: even your name too much your name.

Then where could I pass through,
a cemetery, the great hoard,

every piece of plastic you touched
I held as a child, another

spent wire. What resistance might
we amass in that last field, museum

boned in fabric wrapped your recollection,
from which a hawthorn grew.

Your vessel through the Inside Passage
did not prepare you for the one from Arctic

Wales that blew away. A storm, an ice season,
the aching in your makeshift hut—you should have

followed the custom, stayed warm in the earth.
Nine dozen letters by oil lamp to walk across

the channel, court a companion to the rock.
Who will live to speak of you, to proclaim

you have frozen as you will unfurl.

Rushing circulation shakes you,
you had a father and will never

have him again. Forgetting
the northern constellations,

equations you faltered through
but did not comprehend.

Plain vanilla ice cream, worn-in flannel,
white-crowned sparrow.

What did I do instead of drawing
you into the world? Sang an opera,

six, stayed up past an early bedtime. Let
a story tell me, thinned the pear tree's

inside, witnessed the peach scar over
and set April's buds in January.

Cleaned up my brown leaves and thought,
if the sun returns, it will strike right here.

All this time our mass was a behavior,
not intrinsic. How solid then

our uncertain potential, the probability
we'll orbit each other until decay.

An array emitted from my first note,
my hand quaking everywhere,

the point unknowable.

Even where the real people hadn't walked,
a bird had flown. Eggs tucked in the craggy

plateau and otherwise a sprout of moss,
fissures spanning the compass

to Russia, past the ship receding,
the next rounded eon, invaders discovering

nothing but themselves.

IV

Lay Down Your Rigid Creation

Listen: you are not yourself, you are crowds
of others, you are as leaky a vessel as was
ever made, you have spent vast amounts of
your life as someone else, as people who
died long ago, as people who never lived, as
strangers you never met. . . . There are other
ways of telling.

—Rebecca Solnit

In the tented twilight, triangle of canopy
through the vinyl port, I felt

your blood in my blood, saw you
on your back in the salvaged wood

cabin that first winter in the Bering Strait.
The petrified ivory you scavenged

tucked in your leather briefcase,
seal-shaped inkwell and beaded mukluks,

spoils of a sluggish war.

How many times did you almost see me,
a particle sputtering from the void.

I measure our revolution in steps on the surface,
in shovelsful, in seasons until flowering

and fruit. I found you staring out,
half-cropped café lights in the solstice

night and all your hair—we both know
you haven't looked that way in epochs.

Which of us will welcome leaving life
as from the once-dreamt party.

When the saying ceases, this
dented canoe. Preparing for the day

we could wax static, but we
extinguish. *Paddle,*

promise. The best part about winter
is winter, pause in the dimming chute.

Whatever you do, the wheels will break
away. Tomorrow they rusted out yesterday—

you slept with your not-love waiting
for the eleventh floor, wind river running green.

What is a family, an evening your routes divide,
cigarette smoke and shouts wafting

up from the bars below.

Enough time and you cannot
argue. Acid-strip hydrangeas

blue-purple straggling
our consolation. A stolen

white-blossomed bicycle. Your hands
full of marbles, of button

thread, the heaviest bag of flour
crawling with weevils. How will you

raise the food to your mouth?

After hate lies twine into granite, brine
into mineral creatures made of lace.

On the other side of ice,
invention, your ulu, reindeer fur,

and walrus stomach traded for a crisp
apron. I went on a growing-up adventure, too,

into the hearts of children, where I fear
I'm lodged, all shrapnel and good intention.

Great-grandfather I never knew, your son-in-law
born on Skokomish land I still cross,

city to the razored oyster beds. Everywhere
we've gone to plant our history, the lichen

follows. Crab pot hauling up a giant octopus.
Quonset hut surfing the permafrost

where my father's little hands could not will
a single watermelon to grow. No chance you'd guess

how it would subside, how your sudden exit
would shackle us to rebirth.

The weak graft split overnight,
bangles of unripe apples in the mulch.

There was no resurrection. Nothing to do
but throw away the old tree and move on.

We mark and fuss over the particulars,
but absence begins the lowest rung.

About forty miles from Nome we encountered
the ice. The woman who loved God could question.

He brought her to the island not, in fact,
beatified. *Pieces from fifty to one hundred*

feet long above water. Might drink her away,
his sons, his daughter's son. The names untangle

something in the cells as they tug, St. Michael,
Point Hope.

What recovered from the wayward slicing
dared not form a petal. Half sister, half traitor,

half inhabitant of a borrowed body. The fact is
she returned. Meanwhile, the moon passed

between us. I pictured a glowing circle in the black,
not splashed plasma on a purple midday sky.

Not my trapped sepals metamorphosed
in the sediment, fleeing preservation.

One day, history runs out.
The schematic alone

more than everything you ever toted,
the thought of your acacia grazing

unfamiliar atmosphere. What dark energy you bring
to expand the universe is not yours to inventory.

No more testimony.

What, then, was the nature of light?
The new system hung incommensurate

though it had the same name, as in *marriage*
or *mother*. A ripple of photons

banded at the margin, where we jumped,
one state to another.

I wanted for you the invisible door,
the one you couldn't search for,

the end of your breath's long hallway.

The epigraphs come from Anne Sexton's "Baby Picture," Lucie Brock-Broido's "Bodhisattva," Lucille Clifton's "11/10 again," and Rebecca Solnit's *The Faraway Nearby*.

The italicized text in the poem beginning *"About forty miles from Nome"* comes from a 1908 letter written by my paternal great-grandmother Lois Thompson, on her way by ship from Seattle to Iŋaliq (Little Diomede Island) in the Bering Strait. She accompanied her new husband, my great-grandfather Roy Thompson, a committed socialist who was the first white schoolteacher to make it through the winter on the island and was returning for a second year. Eileen Norbert's beautiful and meticulously researched *Menadelook* (Sealaska Heritage Institute in association with University of Washington Press, 2016) includes descriptions of community life among the Inaliit at that time. Though my great-grandfather went with the express intention to be of service to humankind, the government and missionary school systems left a painful, multigenerational legacy for many Alaska Natives. Launch points for further reading include William L. Iġġiaġruk Hensley's *Fifty Miles from Tomorrow* (Picador, 2010) and Ernestine Hayes's *Blonde Indian* (University of Arizona Press, 2006).

ACKNOWLEDGMENTS

Thank you to the journals in which excerpts from this book first appeared: *8 Poems, Berfrois, can we have our ball back?, Empty Mirror,* and *Parentheses.*

Multiple intersecting indie lit scenes have been my community and inspiration for the last fifteen-plus years, and I'm grateful to all the editors and compatriots who've taken chances on my work and supported me during that time. In particular, thank you to Christian Peet of Tarpaulin Sky and the team at Sidebrow.

A lineage of teachers and mentors extending back to childhood encouraged me to live within language, including Whitney Tjerandsen, Vicki O'Keefe, Joyce Thompson, Stephen Thomas, Les Lessinger, Helene Foley, Saskia Hamilton, Quandra Prettyman, my instructors at Centrum, and my professors at Mills College, particularly my advisors, Stephen Ratcliffe and Elmaz Abinader.

I would not have made it this far without my long-standing writing group—Carly Anne West, Nina LaCour, and Laura

Joyce Davis—or my nonblood family since before conscious memory, Kristen. Much appreciation to Jessica M. and Linda Brice for guiding me and bearing witness as I've woken from old trances.

Eternal gratitude to the National Poetry Series for supporting contemporary poets, judge Carol Muske-Dukes for choosing this collection, and editors Paul Slovak and Allie Merola for believing in it and giving it the gift of careful attention. This book represents the fourth manuscript and eighth time I've submitted to the contest, as well as my third manuscript to be a finalist—and its publication marks the culmination of one of my oldest dreams.

My partner in life, art, and crime, Gregory, has picked me up off the existential pavement too many times to count, dusted me off, and reminded me the process is all we have. Even on the days when I don't love the creative journey, I love him.

Last but certainly not least, love and thanks to my parents, Sylvia and Marvin, who supported my commitment to writing from the earliest days. My late father's relentless genealogical research before the advent of DNA methods lives on through many families' records around the world and shaped my perspective on history and ancestry. My mother instilled in me an artist's sensibility and read me poetry before I was born—I think some part of her has always known where I was headed.

PHOTO BY TERESA K. MILLER

Teresa K. Miller is the author of *sped* and *Forever No Lo* as well as coeditor of *Food First: Selected Writings from 40 Years of Movement Building*. Her poems and essays have appeared in *ZYZZYVA*, *AlterNet*, *Entropy*, *DIAGRAM*, and elsewhere. Originally from Seattle, she graduated from Barnard College and the Mills College MFA program and now tends a mini orchard near Portland, Oregon. Her middle initial is for her great-great-aunt Kate Thompson, a childless adventurer who knew all the birds.

PENGUIN POETS

PENGUIN POETS